T0198900

HALF PAST IN THE A.M.

a conversation amongst selves

Tomisin Oluwole

AuthorHouse™
1663 Liberty Drive
Bloomington, IN 47403
www.authorhouse.com
Phone: 1 (800) 839-8640

Because of the dynamic nature of the Internet, any web addresses or links contained in this book may have changed
since publication and may no longer be valid. The views expressed in this work are solely those of the author and do
not necessarily reflect the views of the publisher, and the publisher hereby disclaims any responsibility for them.

Any people depicted in stock imagery provided by Getty Images are models,
and such images are being used for illustrative purposes only.
Certain stock imagery © Getty Images.

This book is printed on acid-free paper.

ISBN: 978-1-7283-6310-3 (sc)
ISBN: 978-1-7283-6309-7 (e)

Print information available on the last page.

Published by AuthorHouse 05/27/2020

authorHOUSE®

HALF PAST
IN THE A.M.

the brooding solitude of an artist's mind
mystifies the reality that they are simply wallflowers;
eavesdropping on the silent conversation
nature continues to present its pedestrians.

REDEFINITIONS OF LOVE - I

she flickered a light to let him in,
and whispered sweet sounds like barberton
"have you come to save me, save us from hell?"
sunshine, daisies, and a kiss from Elle
no, my love. this right here, this is hell.

REDEFINITIONS OF LOVE - II

hurried strokes and a penchant for intoxication

neon lights illuminate a bleak night

today, we rest

tomorrow, we bask in debauchery.

hold my hand, and count to ten

un deux trois

perhaps, it's me who fell.

EUPHORIA

I've shed my skin,
reptilia, mammalia
And broken my ribs,
for pure ...euphoria

Serenade me with a trumpet and watch my
soul come to life
Feed me with passion and let desire
consume my tides

the urgency in my wanting to see you
has led to the potency in my desire for you

Perhaps there's nothing worse
than being unaware of one's own trauma
Navigating through cobbled
streets littered with puddles
Tears of a pain stricken child
mindlessly loitering in the shadow
of one's depth
Alone but not without
As fear and damage offer the
numb comfort of a misplaced
psyche.

BLAHNIK.

Blood on my Manolo's

You can't tame me.
To think such is more than a mockery,
it's ludicrous.
I can't tame her.
I must be delusional to have thought such,
mad indeed.
She could sense his thoughts, she always
could
The tension in his jaw, the desire in his eyes
His lips betrayed his façade,
They were sensual in the most intimate way,
They were pretty.
She crossed her legs, parted her lips
And took a smoke.
The smell, her presence..
He was all too aroused
Fuck, she was gorgeous
And she was aware.
He was going mental
She was toxic, and she knew it.

He watched her uncross her legs
Then cross them again
A carelessly tactical act
They were just legs,
But they were hers.
I'm thirsty,
Are you going to offer me a drink ?
He flinched
She smirked
I guess not..
Are you satisfied ?
He heard the words but didn't recall seeing
her lips move.
I'm truly insane
She laughed.. she must have sensed his
thoughts again
Suddenly he noticed her heels,
What's that?
Oh, this… I got blood on my Manolo's.

HONEY

Honey, honey, how do you do it?

Barely a touch

Hardly a taste

Yet your senses linger on me.

I'm clinging unto you, but you're the one that sticks

Honey, honey, why do you do this ?

Always a lot but never too much

You entice yet clearly despise me.

I'm a mess, but you're the one I clean up after

Honey, honey, can we do that?

I'll listen

And you'll listen too.

I'm your nectar, but you're so sweet

Honey, honey, I think ..

I'm done.

ME MYSELF & MJ

I don't know you that well
But I know you well enough
We converse for a time
Then part ways till the next
Fleeting encounters
Paired with lasting impressions
You're my soul, you're a lover
You're my poison, you're a stranger

I don't know you that well
But I know of you
Your scent, your taste
How you even like to be cuddled
You're everyone's
Yet no one's
His, hers, and mine

So tell me Mj,
Whose touch do you crave the most ?

Always Sunny in Melrose.

Are you leaving ? Yes
Will you be back soon ?
No

She's hurt.
I always manage to hurt her, but she knows I will. She expects that from me, and
quite frankly I'm too much of a gentleman to let her down, so I play my part. I
watch her hurt.
She's uncertain.
She has been since the day I laid eyes on her. But her uncertainty only arises
when I'm around . She's wary of me. And she should be, I told her so myself.
Oh…I suppose that's for the best, right ?
Right

She's worried.
I never could understand why she worries about me. It's useless. I'm too far
gone, but her pretty little head likes to romanticize my redemption.
So I let her worry, doesn't bother me that she does.

She's scared.
She thinks I'm not coming back but she knows I will. I always do. I don't love her. I tell
her all the time, and she cries…every time. It's exhausting.

Sunny? Yeah?
Silence. She's staring at her bare feet. They're dainty, delicate like her. I like that
about her. I like everything about her. She's my Rose.
She looks up at me. Fuck you Sunny.

ROAD TRIP.

EL DORADO ?

Remember when we took a trip? To El Dorado ? It was brief I admit, and very surreal. But it was El Dorado. Surely you remember.
I drove your dad's Mercedes. The 1961 190SL, fuck she was a beauty. I can't believe he let me, he's crazy.
You kept telling me to drive faster…you're crazy too. And I did, didn't I ? I drove faster for you. And then we stopped at that gas station, the one with the dingy lights and weird flavored Cheetos. I didn't get it, but you didn't care much. So I pretended not to.
I think it was mid-July, was it ? Anyway, it felt like a mid-summer time. Why else would we drive with the sunroof down. We drove for miles and miles, I was exhausted but I had to see El Dorado. We had to see El Dorado.

Remember the trees? Yeah the trees…they looked particularly vibrant. So bloody green and foreign. Hm, they were tropical.
And the days. They just dragged on and on and on. It was perfect. I was in absolute awe but you weren't. I wish you were. Did you try the mangoes? Because I don't remember. I'm pretty sure you didn't. To spite me I bet. You know, you really are something.

You wanted a smoke break after that. It felt like the whole trip was a smoke break, but I didn't want one. I didn't want to sully our paradise. You said I was insane. I thought you were too.

Then I woke up in the back of my red Volkswagen van. Yeah the 1966 one. You were disgusted, I was disappointed. I really did want to go to El Dorado.

Pink Cadillac

If our minds were magnets and our bodies were poles
Would attraction seem real, authentic
Or a figment, merely scientific

If our lips spoke truth and our ears heard meanings
Would our words be careful
Our thoughts still bare their fill

If our fingers were strings and our nails the chords
Would our melodies form new tunes
That linger like lazy afternoons

If our feet were maps, and our soles anchors
Would we explore wide and far
Or remain, capable but fixed as a star

If my eyes were signals, arrows pointing to strewn keys
And your cheeks were mirrors, reflecting the slightest tease of a breeze
Would you drive back,
In my pink Cadillac ?

END.

HALF PAST

IN THE A.M.

How do I care so intently without feeling so deeply?

Why does age strip the white from our eyes

The spark diminished

The curiosity extinguished

Must youth be the elixir that awakens our life

Or perhaps,

Youth is the constant state of mind experienced by all

Yet captured by few,

We know this

Because of the light in their smile

The white in their eyes

A poet's delight is knowing words and passions are one
and the same

A poet's tragedy is hoping sense in sensibility fits in
but a mere frame

Dim the lights down I quiet my thoughts
My mind, a train station refuses to
succumb
Thoughts linger like the forlorn cry of a train long gone
And so,
The night begins

Make Sense
For some reason we tend to associate this simple
clause with intellect…be more intellectual.
The flaw perhaps, is, where's the wits in sense?
The synergy between mind and body, the
mutual admiration amidst flesh and soul; there's
a genius to that. Not within the capacity of
articulating oneself; rather, in the intent and
full grasp of understanding one's many selves.

I played the piano today
My fingers were delicate, agile
My posture poised, perfect
Each note, each key
Encased with my emotions
I was amongst the audience
Watching myself.
Enraptured…how could one feel so
much, pour so much
It was endless
And it was just the beginning

I was soft, I was gentle
I was rough, I was harsh
I was callous in the most tender way
I was a paradox, a spectacle
I suppose I was everyone that night
And like everyone, I felt everything

The audience, my passengers, and I,
the conductor
They had come to feel my sentiments
in hopes of drowning theirs
Shame. I was a scam
I had steered each of them back to
their departure terminal
I had shared all that was already
theirs
My hands held the mirror but their
reflections were unflinching

Why had they come to watch me play?

I was an amateur disguised in the
façade of a composer They listened
to my sounds but I conversed with
their silence
I played the piano today,
Until they felt nothing.

A dozen emotions flood my mind

I try to grasp a hold of one

It's strange

I suppose all I can do is observe

Play the part

Watch the show

Detached yet within the same body

Quiet observations

We take fore granted

A still mind

In a world so active

Responsive yet attentive

We ought,

To listen more

The Day Moon

To be able to write music

Is perhaps the most arduous

Yet delightful art

Vulnerability seeping through the pages

Words forever lingering thoughts

Melodies constant reminders of feelings left unsaid

The result? A body of art

That transcends all art

Yet inspires the art

So you see,

To write music is to be endless

Like the day moon.

I'm spending today with her

But my heart's already leaping at the thought of seeing

her tomorrow.

Let's not forget the sensual curves of her lips

The days seem to blur
Yesterday was last week
And tomorrow's next week.
I'm breezing through the days
Except,
That is indeed all I feel
The wind in my face. Nothing else.

Faces everywhere
I sit and ponder
Is beauty here ?
I truly wonder

10 am and I've already cried my share for the week

Does it ever get easier?

No, apparently not

I'm feeling more empty by the days

And I'm not sure how I feel about that

How to feel about that...

I worry I'm not worrying enough

Yet that's all I seem to be doing

This new emptiness. Could it be peace of mind?

Is my mind so unfamiliar to such that I can hardly identify this feeling?

Perhaps,

It is

I've prayed for this moment, this state for so long

Now I can barely respond to it

Or maybe,

I've felt so much, for too long

And now I'm over it

In the worst way ever,

I'm distancing myself from my reality, and stepping into a blank space
A space too white for my good.
A space of nothing.

1 ≥ 2

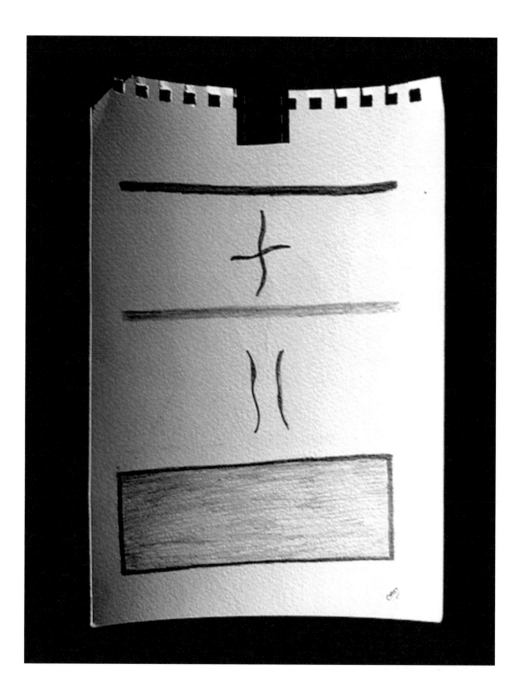

If I let my mind wonder,

Will it only question my existence?

Scrutinize the inner grooves that make all move,

And pick apart the little things, the things we know not true.

I wonder if our existence was made for the sole purpose that one may forever become two.

When the clouds, cloud and the sun barely
peeks through,
where do the lost souls go?
and who do they go there with?

tell me one thing that plagues your mind ?

hands entwine,
a delicate dance by none but lovers.

Pensive

scrunched eyebrows, crystal eyes

a pondering mind

a pensive thought

let in room, let them roam

let your demons come back home

for the homeless lady on Cherry,

she spoke to me of God and man,
she spoke to me of me.
to her I was a beautiful angel that wrote sweet
words, an angel sent to grace these parks
she asked me what I sat and wrote, then christened me a poet.

she told me of the son she birthed, the son she could not raise
she touched upon a life she led, such hearts can't be erased.

she spoke of love, she spoke of light
she spoke of love with so much light

this homeless lady, this lady that dreams alone
came up to me, and asked one thing
one thing, one thing alone.

"To write a poem for her son,"
the one that has her soul.

A collective breath

As we gather our senses

Yours mine theirs, now ours.

Standstill

04.16.2020

Printed in the United States
By Bookmasters